To our dear, bestest friends, Stuart and Karen —
Thank you for your continued love and friendship.

REINVENT YOUR
SABBATH SCHOOL

Discover How [...
a Ministry-driven (...

Chris and Yolanda Blake

Enjoy the journey!
Go with God.
Chris and Yolanda

REVIEW AND HERALD® PUBLISHING ASSOCIATION
HAGERSTOWN, MD 21740

The authors assume full responsibility for the accuracy of all facts
and quotations as cited in this book.

Unless noted otherwise, Bible texts in this book are from
the Revised Standard Version of the Bible, copyright © 1946, 1952,
1971, by the Division of Christian Education of the National Council
of Churches of Christ in the U.S.A. Used by permission.
Texts credited to NIV are from the *Holy Bible, New
International Version.* Copyright © 1973, 1978, 1984, International
Bible Society. Used by permission of Zondervan Bible Publishers.
Texts credited to NKJV are from the New King James Version.
Copyright © 1979, 1980, 1982 by Thomas Nelson, Inc. Used by per-
mission. All rights reserved.

This book was
Edited by Andy Nash
Copyedited by Jocelyn Fay and James Cavil
Cover photo by PhotoDisc
Typeset: 11/14 Cheltenham

PRINTED IN U.S.A.

05 04 03 02 01   5 4 3 2 1

R&H Cataloging Service
Blake, James Christopher, 1951-

    Reinvent your sabbath school: discover how exhilarating
a ministry-driven class can be, by Chris and Yolanda Blake.

    1. Sabbath school.   I. Blake, Yolanda Cervantes.   II. Title.
                            268

ISBN 0-8280-1600-3

Dedication

First, this book is dedicated to our sons,
Nathanael and Geoffrey,
and to our soon-to-be daughter-in-law, Andrea.

May you always be active
in the Sabbath school of your choice.

Second, we dedicate this edition to the members
of Something Else. Without you this book—
and the realistic hope it brings—would never
have witnessed the light of day.

Thank you for your incredible love.

Contents

Preface

"What's your uncle's name?" asks the man at the front of the room.

"Steven."

The man at the front writes on a whiteboard "9. Steven—brain cancer—" and turns to face the class. "Cancer is an epidemic, isn't it? I can't remember two weeks when we haven't prayed for someone with cancer. Who will pray for Steven?"

A hand raises.

"Thank you, Anita." He writes "Anita" beside the prayer request.

Another voice: "Do you think Steven would like a card?"

Steven's niece considers this. "Yes," she says at last, "I think he would."

A box filled with pens and cards is passed to her. Steven's card ("We are praying for you") and a pen join two other cards being passed around the class to be signed and mailed that day.

"Are there any more requests or expressions of gratitude? . . . Any follow-ups to past requests? . . . All right, then, we'll start with Mark, and after Anita I'll pray for the remainder of our classtime. Let's pray."

Heartfelt prayers ascend from across the room: for a principal in a coma; a young boy hit by a car; a student struggling with depression; a lost pair of glasses; a time of transition for elderly parents; appreciation for all this class does; an upcoming wedding; a book being written; Steven with brain cancer.

As happens every week, prayer time ends nearly 25 minutes after it began.

This is Sabbath school.

It's another prayer time. A friend requests prayer for Cindy, single mother of three, who is a member of the class but isn't here this morning. She's too discouraged. Her sputtering car gave out on Thursday and was officially declared dead on Friday. That day two sets of parents called Cindy, threatening to remove their three children from her child-care business if she couldn't pick them up. Without the income from these families, Cindy's family cannot reasonably survive.

The class decides to delay the current money ministry project and concentrates instead on Cindy's needs. In addition to praying for her, the class raises $875 that morning.

On Sunday a church member sells his car for $875 to Cindy.

On Monday Cindy drives her newly acquired car to pick up all the children, keeping her business intact.

This is Sabbath school.

At 10:45 on the first Sabbath morning of each month, 10 people enter Matt Talbot Kitchen and begin putting together a meal to serve 65 homeless and needy people. The 10 volunteers are children, teenagers, and adults from churched and nonchurched backgrounds. For the next two hours they will pray, prepare, cook, serve, smile, talk, and clean up. Lives are touched on both sides of the counter. People who formerly thought of church as "impractical" eagerly look forward to their next opportunity to serve.

This is Sabbath school.

"Jonah 3:3," announces the teacher, "says that Nineveh was 'an exceedingly great city, three days' journey in breadth.' Yet we know precisely how 'great' the old city was because its ruined walls are still visible. If you look at the map on the whiteboard, you can see that the city was about three miles long and a mile across. So how do you reconcile 'three days' journey' with the actual distances? Then in the next verse Jonah 'began to go into the city, going a day's journey.' What do you make of this? Was Jonah just an *awfully* slow walker?"

Lively discussion ensues. The class comes to realize that this distance must have measured how long it took Jonah to walk by every house on every street.

The teacher asks, "What does this tell us about evangelism today?"

"It means that we ought to measure our evangelism in terms of physically touching every household," responds one class member. "Jonah could have walked into the middle of the city within a half hour, made his pronouncement, and left. But those types of information transmissions don't truly change people. God wants us to enter individual lives to bring about repentance and healing. God desires that we dialogue."

This is Sabbath school.

———————

"Before my membership was transferred to this church, I knew few people here," says Carole. "This class involved me from the first day. I was able to pray for people I didn't know, and I learned names when they were put up on the board. When we each took a package to mail for prison ministries or I wrote out a check for something I passionately believed in, I was already making a contribution and getting integrated. People can get involved even if they don't hold a membership here.

"When my husband is traveling I always have a place to go, because the class sponsors a weekly potluck in members' homes. I get to know these people on a deeper level as a result. The class has provided an anchor and made my new home a wonderful place to live.

"I've been here only a year, and I know this class would do anything for me."

This is Sabbath school.

Chapter One

Each Journey Begins With a Step:

"How About . . . Something Else?"

IF YOU'VE BEEN in the Seventh-day Adventist Church long, you've probably endured one. In it you've squirmed and stifled a yawn. You've checked the clock on the wall and hoped that it was truly "later than we think." You've cringed and smoldered through a "lesson study" that was in fact a thinly veiled, interminable sermon or a wandering gripe session or a round of fill-in-the-blanks that relied entirely on quick, smug, simplistic answers. You've wondered how anything in God's creation could be so removed from real life.

You've asked yourself why you bother coming to Sabbath school at all.

And yet you know that most Sabbath school leaders and participants are well-meaning, dedicated followers of the same Saviour you worship. How does this scenario keep happening on a weekly basis?

Actually, that isn't the important question. There's another more vital question all of us need to ask:

Is this what Jesus had in mind?

We don't think so.

Ellen White didn't think so either. In the August 1, 1892, issue of *Sabbath School Worker* she writes, "The great want in our Sabbath school work is the want of the light of life. . . . How sad it is to think of the great amount of mechanical work that is done in the Sabbath school, while there is little evidence that there is moral transformation in the souls of those who teach and who are taught."

Some may claim that Sabbath school is a relic, an archaic reference to a bygone era. They ask, "Why do we need Sabbath school in the new millennium, anyway?"

Jesus answered that question after His resurrection when He stated, "All authority in heaven and on earth has been given to me. Go therefore and *make disciples* of all nations, baptizing them in the name of the Father and of the Son and of the Holy Spirit, *teaching them* to observe *all* that I have commanded you; and lo, *I am with you always,* to the close of the age" (Matthew 28:18-20, RSV).

In the centuries since those words were uttered, many Christians have missed Jesus' meaning. Beyond our baptizing believers—we often call this making decisions—He said that we must make disciples. A huge task. Especially in a fast-paced, virtual reality age—especially during the week—finding the time to dig deeply and create disciples gets harder and harder.

However, the genius of the Sabbath school slot for Adventists is that *Saturday morning is the one time we can count on people to show up.* What better hour exists for us as Christ's followers to deal collectively with present and eternal realities?

The good news is that it can happen. Even better news is that it is happening.

Beth, an exercise physiologist, says, "I hadn't been very involved in church for 12 years. This Sabbath school brought me back because it really lives out the lessons of Jesus."

Sig, a tennis pro and a Lutheran, relates, "I like the way this class reaches into the actual lives of people. I hate to miss a Sabbath!"

Dale, an audio equipment designer, notes, "This is like a little piece of heaven on earth. It's a community that acts on its beliefs and cares about each other in surprising ways."

All these quotes, and the rest of the quotes in this book, describe only one Sabbath school class. The five vignettes in the preface originate from the same class, and perhaps most amazing, all of them can happen in any given week.

MINISTRY-DRIVEN (MD) SABBATH SCHOOLS: JUST WHAT THE GREAT PHYSICIAN ORDERED

As the Protestant Reformation rediscovered old truths, so a Sabbath school reformation rediscovers truths for our day, healing truths that hearken back to the Adventist pioneers and Acts believers. Dr. Luke records that the early Christian church "devoted themselves to the apostles' teaching and fellowship, to the breaking of bread and the prayers . . . and distributed [goods] to all, as any had need" (Acts 2:42-45).

Sabbath school is the heartbeat of your church. What the heart is to the physical body, the Sabbath school is to the church body. If the Sabbath school throbs with the spirit of prayerful Bible study, harmony, and practical missionary activity, the church will possess the same elements." Ellen White writes in *Counsels on Sabbath School Work:* "The influence growing out of Sabbath school work should improve and enlarge the church. . . . There is a most precious missionary field in the Sabbath school" (p. 9).

A ministry-driven Sabbath school points toward Christ and is propelled by five ministries: prayer, money, time, study, and social. In this book we'll share a case history of our ministry-driven class—its inception, growth, failures and strengths, and how you can begin your own. This class was featured in both Sabbath school sessions at the 2000 General Conference session in Toronto.

But first, a few essential points.

1. This model isn't for everybody. Not everyone in your church will want to participate in a class this practical and personal. Some members desire to study the lesson for the entire class period; others have all their needs met just fine where they are, thank you. Many are not ready just yet to leave a comfort zone. Often as Christians we expect others to "get" in 20 minutes what we took 20 years to learn. Be patient. Be charitable. And be as tenacious as Jacob wrestling at the Jabbok to stay in touch with your God.

2. Adapt these ideas to your specific circumstances. Use the spiritual gifts of your members to sculpt the fresh outlines for your own Sabbath school. If you're still reading these words right now, you're interested enough to consider making changes on Saturday morning that will affect the entire week, every week. Be creative. It comes with being made in the image of the Creator.

3. Begin with a core of committed, positive, risk-taking believers who love God. The core group may be three to four people; the group may be 14 to 18 years old; the group may come from widely different backgrounds. Whatever the case, your core must be unified in loving Jesus out of gratitude for His salvation. The group must be unified also in loving the supreme objects of God's affection—all human beings, with all their problems and faults.

4. Pray with all your heart, mind, soul, and strength. God knows you need it. Pray and listen closely. Pray and work hard. Pray and be at peace.

5. Get ready for a spiritual adventure. You will be energized with hope and wonder, gum-swallowing depth and tearful warmth. God is always surprising. Hold on for the ride when God becomes the pilot.

STARTING OVER

In the fall of 1994 Pastor Greg Nelson, of the College View Seventh-day Adventist Church in Lincoln, Nebraska, asked Chris if he might be interested in starting a Sabbath school class. "Some people are wanting a new class," Greg explained, "and your name was mentioned as a leader. Anyway, a room just opened up— what do you think?"

What do we think? We thought a lot about the possibilities. We thought that we weren't interested in another "business as usual" Sabbath school. We thought that we were tired of *talking* about Christian ministry— we wanted to *do* it. We thought that Sabbath school should be greatly anticipated and more fun than a dripping faucet. We thought that maybe we were crazy enough to give it a try.

First, of course, we had to think of a name. Already a thriving twentysomething class existed, as well as a thirty-fortysomething class, along with other classes. So we decided to call our class Something Else. At least we would get those who might say offhandedly, "Let's try something else today."

In the beginning Something Else was largely without form and void of purpose except for two distinctive margins. Inside these margins everything would fall:

A. "The kingdom of God does not consist in talk but in power" (1 Corinthians 4:20). Too often Sabbath school is all talk and no power. That would change here.

B. "Christianity is always intensely practical" (*Messages to Young People,* p. 200). Too often Sabbath schools are intensely *im*practical—a weekly convergence of the weakly theoretical. That would change too.

So in January 1995, we set up 35 chairs in a small room and began to grow in godly ways. In our first few weeks we averaged about 15 attendees. Then attendance doubled, interest swelled, and miracles began to happen. We did have our share of troubles, of course.

But that's another chapter.

Chapter two

Growing Pains:

"We Haven't Done a Thing!"

"When I came here I felt spiritually dead and depressed. I was on edge almost constantly. Since I came to the Something Else class my spiritual life has vastly improved, and I feel as though a great burden has been lifted off my shoulders. I praise God for this class."

"Overall the class has been a good experience for me. I do travel a lot, and at times I do get the feeling that it really does not matter whether I am there or not or if I am missed if I do not come. It is my understanding that the class is working on structure to make sure that missed members are remembered."

SOMETHING ELSE WAS always primed for moving. Moving from our comfort zones. Moving into the real-life community. Moving by the Holy Spirit. And, eventually, moving out of our cramped, noisy room.

Any growth is at times uncomfortable; to believe otherwise is to be deluded. Those who cling to comfort "no matter what" inevitably make comfort their god. They miss the reward of the risk-taking servants Jesus described in Matthew 25. What's the reward?

The joy.

From the beginning "the joy" has been a central component of our Sabbath school. We believe Psalm 16 when it states, "In [God's] presence there is fullness of joy." We agree with George MacDonald when he writes, "It is the heart that is not yet sure of its God that is afraid to laugh in His presence."

Moreover, we have found that we may experience joy no matter what the circumstances. As Madeleine L'Engle points out: "The difference between happiness and joy is sorrow."

And so we take godly risks. We do it for joy; we do it for Jesus.

To be alive is to take risks. We don't want to be afraid of mistakes to the point that we can do nothing great. Fearful people desire only to make it to the grave safely. Day by day, they suffer through a perpetual "near-life" experience. The Bible, on the other hand, proclaims, "There is no fear in love, but perfect love casts out fear" (1 John 4:18).

We have made blunders as we have grown, and we believe our church ought to be honest about its mistakes. Honestly, we have been Spirit-led even through the lapses. The following is meant to give you hope—and to show that the ministry-driven road is rarely smooth and easy.

FEARSOME FOURSOME

As we started our new class, a few (not many) rumors began taking off. Our church has been superbly supportive of us, but anyone trying to do *something else* to actually influence real life will create misgivings and suspicion.

"They don't study the lesson."

"They're splitting off. They want to be their own church."

"They think they're better than other Sabbath schools."

We kept our eyes on the prize and kept running the good, true race of faith. Eventually the few critics quieted when the complaints proved over time to be untrue.

Bigger difficulties arose from our own making. These problems appeared in four forms:

1. Time crunch. Even with an hour slot (a luxury to many Sabbath schools, we know) we had trouble fitting in all the opportunities that appeared each week. We decided to start a few minutes earlier.

But we still ran overtime. Moreover, parents needed to leave early to pick up their young children, and thereby missed the conclusion of the study. Coming at the end, the lesson was being regularly squeezed by the other ministries. Some people left, grumbling, "There's not enough study time."

We considered switching the study ministry with an earlier ministry, but we didn't want to miss out on those ministries either. Eventually we developed a time schedule:

10:01-10:25   **Prayer ministry**
10:26-10:41   **Money, time, and social ministries**
10:42-11:05   **Study ministry**

This successfully created more time for our study.

Still, we had no spot for music (although we occasionally end our study with a song or hymn). We tried starting class 15 minutes early with praise singing but, because we are split between two services, after a few weeks attendance dwindled. We decided that we couldn't afford the time for music, especially since we sing so much during church service. Other ministry-driven classes, however, successfully start with singing.

2. Involving everyone. The key to a healthy body is involvement. Any body member cut off from circulation will atrophy and lose life.

Our class goal is to involve every member in meaningful ministry, yet we haven't always enabled everyone to "own" the class—thereby hurting the overall impact of our ministries.

In his frustration a former time ministries leader declared to a group of members at a potluck, "We talk about doing all these things, but we haven't done a *thing!*" His charge seemed unjustified to people who had previously been in Sabbath schools that didn't do one tenth what we were doing.

To a degree, though, he was right. We needed to scale back our aims.

As Yolanda once said: "Even Jesus couldn't save everybody." We can't save *anybody;* we can't *help everybody,* either. A reasonable approach is best. The road paved exclusively with good intentions will turn out to be hard and hot. Ellen White comments that people "in responsible positions should undertake no more than they can do thoroughly, promptly, and well" *(Testimonies,* vol. 5, p. 415).

3. Members slipping through cracks. Something Else has always carried a passion for being an inclusive class, in which each missing member is truly missed—and knows it. About three years ago we appraised our strengths and weaknesses for "discipleship strategies." Here's how the appraisal looked:

Weaknesses:
1. Visitors aren't immediately assimilated.
2. No recordkeeping of class members.
3. "Maintenance" is pathetic.
4. Not every member is presently involved in meaningful ministry.
5. Not enough small groups.

Strengths:
1. Greeters exist.
2. Willingness.

Not a pretty picture, so we determined to straighten it. Our aims now:

Attendance is recorded weekly.

Members' picture board is regularly checked.

Leaders are given "cell groups" to keep track of.

Greeters foster culture of friendliness.

Friendship dinners take place each Sabbath.

Produce a class brochure, keep Web site updated.

Bring back newsletter.

Create a prayer chain via e-mail.

Conduct in-class interviews.

Enlarge number of social ministry participants.

We're still refining this list, and probably always will be. Times change, people change, resources and needs change. That's all right; God doesn't mind change. As Oswald Chambers comments, "What men call the process, God calls the end."

4. Feeling fresh-squeezed. In our tiny lemon slice of a room we competed each Sabbath with a neighboring multimedia production and, sometimes, a rehearsing choir. Often our prayers coincided with loud "heavenly voices," or so we told ourselves. Members and visitors stopped at the door, peered in at the lack of empty seats, and left. The scene irked us deeply.

At one point Pastor Terry Bock and Chris made an attempt to switch spaces with a much smaller class meeting in a slightly larger room. The two men visited this class to present our case. Both retreated quickly with verbal arrows protruding from their backs.

We hung in there. After a few years, amazingly, a much better room opened up. Here we could seat 80, and after another year we were able to fix it up the way we wished. After we raised money, purchased chairs and (virtually donated) window coverings, lowered the ceiling, installed efficient lighting, tacked up a whiteboard and bulletin boards, stripped an outdated nature mural from the west wall, painted and painted, we were ready. Now if we could just get the air-conditioning to work . . .

Many of you will battle space limitations in your church. "Sorry, no rooms are available" will resonate in your ears. Remember that Joseph and Mary heard the same refrain; rest assured that somehow God will find a way—some "stable" place for a good, if not glorious, beginning.

No matter what the obstacle, God is with you. He can bring out of any annoyance, concern, or predicament a path that demonstrates again the constant watchwords of Christianity: something better.

Chapter Three

Prayer Ministry:

Who Will Pray for Katie?

"Unless you have experienced it, it's hard to appreciate the impact of having someone else in the class pray specifically for your request. It is at once both humbling and strengthening. This is an environment where I know I am valued by others and by God."—Brett Robinson.

"The first time I attended this class I was unprepared for the overwhelming sense of the Holy Spirit during the prayer ministry time and the feeling of awe of what all was being done during the money ministry time. I knew right away that I wanted to be a part of this."—Kim Lee.

PRAYER MINISTRY IN Something Else began the first time we met. The strength and unity this ministry brought to the class is fundamental, enabling, and powerful; nothing can take its place. Prayer connects us with reality. We begin each class period with prayer.

When Something Else started with 15 members, our prayer time lasted 15-20 minutes. Now, with more than 60 members, we take about 25 minutes. One of the first prayers we recall was five years ago when a new member requested that the class pray for him because he had just been diagnosed with prostate cancer. He was to undergo surgery the following week.

Every person in the class got up out of our chairs, knelt around Marlyn, and prayed, hands on shoulders, arm in arm. Marlyn remembers, "I found a fellowship that totally changed my outlook on life. The peace I felt that moment was indescribable." Thankfully, Marlyn's surgery went well, and he is an active member of our class to this day. The following Sabbath we created a 15-foot banner for class members to sign and then delivered it to him in the hospital. We don't want to *stop* at prayer; we act out our impressions from God.

An important part of prayer ministry is our sequence. First the prayer leader asks for requests and prayers of thanks. If someone requests that we pray for Katie, for example, who is experiencing pregnancy complications, the leader writes, "1. Katie" on the whiteboard for all to see. The leader asks clarifying questions, summarizes the nature of the problem, and describes what, *precisely,* we are praying for. This pushes us beyond a stereotypical request that God "be with" someone—the type of prayer that applies universally but lacks personality and depth.

"Does Katie have immediate family with her?"

"Yes, her husband."

"And his name is . . . ?"

"Dave."

"We're praying then for Katie and Dave [writes Dave's name]. They are probably scared right now, so along with her physical healing we'll pray for their emotional healing, that God will grant them His hope and peace.* God longs to heal in so many ways. Please mention in your prayer their unborn child as well. Who will pray for Katie, Dave, and their baby?"

The prayer volunteer will then have his or her name written next to the request. A list usually consists of seven to 10 prayers. Our one guideline is that you cannot pray for your own request. Of course, about half the class does not feel comfortable praying out loud publicly. That's all right. Still, they *participate* by silently lifting their prayers to a merciful God.

During our prayer time we find ourselves on a roller coaster of emotions. We laugh; we cry; we are stunned to silence. The volunteers pray in order, finishing with the leader praying for our class and our time together.

We also keep a box filled with cards to send to people whom we think would like to know that we are praying for them. Various members of the class have donated cards that have been categorized—get well, sympathy, thinking of you, congratulations—along with blank cards for any occasion. The box is passed to the person who made the request, a card is chosen and passed around (with pen attached) for members of the class to sign. The person who first made the request then mails or delivers the card. Again, this is done only if the person receiving it would benefit from a card.

Prayer ministry creates trust, breadth, and openness. Too often Adventists visit a Sabbath school only to keep their deepest joys and needs buried. They arrive at church and leave without one soul knowing what sort of week they had, what challenges they face, what thanks they wish to trumpet. This is dreadfully wrong.

As a result of this sequence of prayer ministry, our class members actually learn who each other is and how our lives are materializing. Moreover, we discover personal needs we can meet through money and time ministries. Many Sabbaths we stop right in the midst of prayer requests to organize visible help. Why wait?

This past year we've begun an e-mail prayer chain so that we don't even have to wait till Sabbath to know needs and lift them up to God. With about 50 addresses on the list, we also touch many class members who serve in children's divisions but who still want to stay in touch.

Even children are touched by our praying. Anita reflects:

"I still today get excited (as I'm sure Christ does) when we hear a person is healed or is at peace with God. I feel I *have* made a difference in the past two years. My daughter Megan knows we pray both on Sabbath and through the week via e-mail. One day she came to me and said, 'My friend Elizabeth is very sick, and the doctors don't know what's wrong. Can we send an e-mail to your friends at Something Else so they can pray?' So the e-message was sent. How pleased I am that my daughter knows the power of prayer through this class."

The prayer ministry is open to all and sends a message of acceptance to all participants. Cindy says, "I enjoy knowing that I can come to a Sabbath school class and share joys and sorrows without being looked down upon or judged. Also, I have a sister who is not an Adventist, who has come to our class to visit. If she has a concern she will call me and say, 'I need you to pray about it for me in your Sabbath school class.' She has seen firsthand in our class the power in prayer."

Vicki, another active member, observes, "My mother, who lives 700 miles away, feels a part of this class—from the cards we've sent when she's had surgery and even when her little dog died. She told me that she cried when she got the card—it meant a lot to her." In response to one of the cards we sent to Vicki's mother, Polly, she wrote, "I loved your card! Life is made up of little things like smiles, kindness, and the hearts of friends."

SHOWING IS BELIEVING

One of the wonderful things about our class is the diversity of people. We enjoy a wide spectrum of ages, talents, and backgrounds, but we are all there to experience God's love for us. Al, who was raised Roman Catholic and is not a member of the Adventist Church, says:

"One of the most impressive aspects of Something Else is how I've been welcomed into this class, though I'm not a member. I thought maybe I'd be on the out-skirts, maybe not quite welcomed in like some of the others, but that's been furthest thing from the truth. I've learned a lot of things, and we've helped a lot of people. We also pray for people in need, no matter who they are. We prayed for my brother, who has chronic alcoholism, and within three weeks he checked himself into a rehab center. Right now he has 60 days' sobriety. To me, that's a miracle."

Stories like Al's, of course, make us wonder why we're not on our knees more. Why we aren't inviting more people to a place where prayers are taken seri-ously, and God's comfort is felt.

We should tell you right here that our class typi-cally runs about an hour and 10 minutes with 25 min-utes spent on prayer ministry, so we have had a few people criticize us for spending too much time on prayer. Individuals have stopped attending our class because they wanted more lesson time.* To be fair, more times than not they attended the class only once or twice; they didn't experience the full impact of prayer ministry—where class members feel a need and bring it to the class, where people get to know each other on a personal and caring level, where we find ourselves looking out for each other even during the week.

When Chris attended the ConneXions99 conference at the General Conference building, he shared with young adults his dream of starting "activist Sabbath schools" across our denomination. Ten people showed up in a small conference room to glimpse this dream and discuss its implications. After starting with a five-minute introduction and initial description of prayer ministry, however, Chris could see that he was making little impact on the listeners. Their eyeballs had glazed over with Nickelodeon TV stares.

"OK," he said, "let's *do* it now. Are there any requests or prayers of thanks?" Marker in hand, he approached a whiteboard.

Twenty minutes later the group had changed dramatically. In those few minutes they had become a community of faith—revealing, redemptive, responsive. Their eyes shone with wonder.

"Wow," said one person, "now I see what you mean."

Merely *talking* to others about the ministries in this book will never suffice. They must *do* to become believers. That's what becoming disciples is all about. That's what the Great Physician ordered.

Prayer will always be a top priority for us. As Tammy, who has since moved to another state, put it: "The most awesome thing about the class was the fact that you could bring *anything* to the class that was important to you to pray about, no matter how trivial it might seem, and the power of prayer was evident week after week in so many different situations."

We live in a world of hurting people and thankful people. Prayer connects us to these people. Somehow prayer enables God and ennobles us. The Bible declares, "The Lord is at hand. Have no anxiety about anything, but in everything by prayer and supplication with thanksgiving let your requests be made known to God" (Philippians 4:5, 6).

So we do.

---

* In cases involving accident or abuse, we pray for the perpetrator as well.

⁺ We have also extended the lesson time by holding "potgoodlucks" in people's homes, with a discussion extension of the lesson.

Chapter Four

Money Ministry:

"I'm So Glad There's Somewhere to Go for Help"

"Mere words seem inadequate to express our gratitude. Your actions are an answer to prayer as I believed God would take care of our finances this month. I am overwhelmed and amazed at the kindness shown to us."

"Jim and I have so much to be thankful for—among them you. You all sent money, blankets, toys, clothes, so much. The thought still brings a tear to my eye. You are angels among us, and my family and I will be forever grateful."

MONEY MINISTRY HAS astounded us. We had no idea that this second ministry would create so much goodwill, so much tearful evidence of God's miraculous leading.

Perhaps it's best in this section to share also what *we've* received, so we'll intersperse letters from a few *recipients* of money ministry. Some are members of our class; most aren't.

"Thank you from the bottom of my heart for what you did. I was so overwhelmed when Paul told me how much you collected; I was just speechless. I'm always

afraid you're going to get sick of me because I'm always on the receiving end and you'll want to throw me out of class, but you always help, even when I don't ask."

The premise of money ministry is to put a face on our giving and to make an immediate impact. Church giving doesn't always need to be faceless and fathomless. We know precisely where the special offering is headed, and we know that we're making a tangible, practical difference every Sabbath. We sometimes hear what a difference it makes in others' lives; we *always* know what a difference it makes in ours.

"I don't know who you are or who sent me a monetary gift—a tangible way of saying that you love me. . . . Thank you so much for thinking about me and giving me your love."

"We get to see the children in their new clothing, with their happy smiles. Your acts of kindness speak an important message about your commitment in caring for God's children who are less fortunate. You are a good example for all of us."

The money ministry process begins with a need, sometimes by request, sometimes just by seeing a need and meeting it.

"How does a person even begin to thank you for what you have done for me? There are no words to describe what's in my heart.

"I can think of no reason my misfortune would matter to anybody. Especially something as 'minor' as vandal-

ism—it wasn't life-threatening or anything 'important.' To think anyone would care about that was so unbelievable. When I received your card in the mail, I was so touched. The card alone meant that much to me.

"Not expecting anything else in the card, I must tell you, the generous gift you included left me speechless. I literally lost my breath. . . . You would've laughed if you saw my reaction. I still cannot believe anyone would do such a thing for me. . . . Thank you all so much. You touched my life!"

A typical request will arrive during the week when someone calls Chris or Paul Richardson, our money ministries leader. A young family needs grocery assistance. Flood victims need help. A college student needs medical services. The need is brought before our class during the money ministry time, right after prayer ministry.

"During the money ministry time my little becomes a lot. This is when as a team we can make a difference to one or many. The idea of a class member bringing a request helps us to feel like the leader of a mission trip. Voting on projects makes the class as a whole the governors. I could never as a single parent afford to give a family a Christmas, but as part of the team of Something Else I am able to do that. Christ would have done this: 'What you do to the least of these, you do for Me.'"

When Paul stands before the class, he alerts us to the money need:

"We were informed this week of a young couple who need a utility bill paid. They are not going to require help again, apparently, but they are in a difficult transition time. The bill is $146. We currently have $74 in our Good Samaritan fund. What is your pleasure?"

At this point the class asks questions and may make suggestions as to how else we might help as more needs become known:

"Do they have any other pressing needs?"

"Not that I know of," says Paul.

"Let's help them with this bill, then."

"So I'm hearing you say," Paul summarizes, "that you want to pay the $146, using up the rest of the Good Samaritan fund. [Heads nod.] All right, here are our two envelopes: one for this special project, and one for regular Sabbath school expense."

"Thank you very much for your generous donation of materials to our religious library. The men at our institution are very excited about having access to good study materials, and I'm sure that they will be put to good use. May the Lord bless you and guide you."—a correctional facility chaplain.

"Thank you for coming to the rescue of this school in Pakistan. What joy you've brought to the school personnel so they can continue to serve young people."

After the envelopes are handed around, Paul takes them outside and counts how much we gave to both. At the end of each Sabbath school he stands and gives a quick report:

"Thank you for your generous offering today. For the special project you gave $193. That means we can pay off the utility bill, and we still have $121 in the Good Samaritan fund for future projects. Your offering for

Sabbath school expense was $28. Thank you for these dollars of hope."

The Good Samaritan fund was a fund established to take care of needs that must be met during the week or unspecified needs for the future.

Our church has graciously allowed the class to maintain a Something Else account. We haven't slacked off of our regular offerings (they have increased, in fact), and the church recognizes the superb impact this ministry is making. Each fourth and fifth Sabbath of the month we pass around just one envelope for Sabbath school expenses.

On Monday the church secretary, Ardis Bullock, makes out a check for $146 to either the utilities company or the recipients. At times we have made payments directly to the company.

"I was looking for a Sabbath school—one where my values and spiritual needs were met. The first day at Something Else—when the five ministries were explained—I offered a prayer of thanksgiving because I felt at home. I was looking for a place where I could be a missionary in my own church. I loved the idea of cooking a meal for the homeless in my town one Sabbath a month—that showed me that this group of people were risk-takers. They also actually helped people out financially. This went along with Ellen White's idea of 'Christianity is always intensely practical.'

"Each week I am part of a team to grow, learn, and love. I have brought my brothers—they both wish they had a Sabbath school like mine where they live, because everyone feels at home here even when they come the first time. It takes a dedicated group of people to make it look effortless."

God has led us every step of the way. On an average Sabbath we each give two or three dollars, but over these five and a half years the class has collected more than $47,000 to fund 141 projects. (See list of projects following this chapter.) When Tim Simon was the money ministries leader he began in his detail-oriented, itemized way to keep track of where our money has gone. This recordkeeping has enabled us to marvel at what God has done through our small group.

One caution: Start small, and let God lead. To begin, emphasize projects less than $100. When Something Else began money ministsries, we required many weeks to raise the initial $350 for the project. Four of our first six projects totaled $60 or less, however.

PRINCIPLES OF MONEY MINISTRY

Money ministry operates on five principles:

1. Money ministry is a participatory process—it's the members' money, not the leaders'.

2. Acts 2—we give first priority to needs presented by class members.

3. Projects from outside the Sabbath school class need to have a class sponsor to be seriously considered.

4. Limited, short-term financial help is what we offer to anyone in need.

5. Prayer for God's leading is what we prefer to do before giving.

"Though I don't belong to your church, I called a member of your class because I heard that you helped people in need. I'm so glad to know that there's a place where someone can go for help."

Amazingly, the class has risen to every money challenge. Many Sabbaths we sit in awe of what God has done. We don't care where people are in need or who they are—we are driven by our love to help.

Some final thoughts on money ministry:

"From the time I came to this class, I felt a part of the family. I was here in Lincoln only a few months and had gone to the class several weeks when I was overwhelmed by a wonderful gift. It was Christmas. I was getting ready to move into a less expensive apartment with my three children, and I had no money to move or for Christmas. The class helped cover the rental deposit and gave me $400 for Christmas. It didn't stop there, though. I've had financial help so many times, and have received prayer for my family members and myself on numerous occasions."

"Generous Sabbath school class, thank you so much for your gift of $144 for Southwestern Adventist University's student aid fund. Your gift has been credited to the tuition/textbook account of a management major here."

"When I first came to Lincoln, my two teenage daughters were—for lack of a better word—horrible. They were into everything that could possibly keep a parent awake at night or give a parent nightmares. The first time I brought them to Matt Talbot Kitchen to help feed some of the homeless in Lincoln, they were impressed, and somehow (only by the grace of God) they slowly came around. My 21-year-old, who now has a baby of her own, comes to class with me; my 18-year-old has also turned over a new leaf. And it was the class who helped.

If it hadn't been for their work, for each individual's prayers, for their caring, it would not have happened. I know, without a single doubt, that they would not be where they are; in fact, neither one of them would probably be alive."

"As a nurse I had a patient, a young mother, who was very ill and was so sad she could not give her family any Christmas presents. I came to Something Else with this request. Not only did we collect $200, but two of the ladies said they would make cookies for her. When these two brought to the hospital the Christmas cookies they had made for her she was so excited and cried because she 'did not know people even cared anymore.' A few days later, after shopping with the money, she and I wrapped packages, and tears again fell. 'Thank you,' was all she could say. When she was up and active again after rehab she came to visit me at the hospital one day. She said to me, 'I will always look for others who might need my help as I can give it. You showed me how.'"

Something Else Sabbath School Money Ministries
(January 1995–September 2000)

COMPLETED PROJECTS
1. $350   to Center for Abused Women
2. $440   in clothing for Union College (UC) students
3. $30   in lenses for UC student
4. $40   to young couple for Thanksgiving
5. $25   donation to Matt Talbot Kitchen
6. $60   two griddles for Matt Talbot Kitchen

7.	$484	cash and donated goods for Christmas 1995 gifts to two Lincoln families
8.	$165	75 loaves of bread to College View Church (CVC) community
9.	$45	two Bibles for two summer campers
10.	$150	for electric/heat bills and grocery certificates for Lincoln family
11.	$90	heat/electric bills paid for Lincoln family
12.	$80	to UC student for two coats and a pair of slacks
13.	$90	textbooks for single mom attending college
14.	$100	to UC student toward medical expenses for infant son
15.	$194	toys for Romanian orphanage
16.	$73	to Lincoln woman to help offset monthly expenses
17.	$200	to Lincoln family whose home was destroyed by fire
18.	$15	to UC student for medical prescription
19.	$50	to UC student who was robbed on the way to Lincoln
20.	$175	toward fees for October Kansas-Nebraska Women's Retreat
21.	$75	to Lincoln family for Thanksgiving
22.	$782	cash and donated goods for Christmas 1996 gifts to two Lincoln families
23.	$75	to UC student who had car broken into
24.	$300	for Christmas gifts, etc., to CVC member
25.	$150	applied toward electrical bill for Lincoln family
26.	$75	to a UC student for Christmas
27.	$125	to a UC single mom for Christmas
28.	$250	to Project Uplift for Cambodia's ethical foundation
29.	$150	to Lincoln/Lancaster Mediation Center for violence-prone youth

30.	$115	to a UC student's family at a time of child's illness
31.	$60	applied to utility bill of Lincoln person with cancer
32.	$50	to a Russian family adapting to America
33.	$300	to a UC student's family at a time of child's illness
34.	$220	to an international student traveling home after 11 years away
35.	$300	to victims of Grand Forks, North Dakota, flood
36.	$150	to a UC student who had an accident and couldn't work
37.	$150	to a UC student, single parent, needing food money
38.	$550	to help in building a deck/ramp for a woman with cancer
39.	$210	to help a woman needing help with her electric bill
40.	$38	to a UC student needing medical services
41.	$1,325	to seven families at Christmas 1997
42.	$200	to families served by the Good Neighbor Center
43.	$360	to Peru mission trip volunteers
44.	$224	to help single mom with transportation expenses
45.	$875	to help another single mom with transportation needs
46.	$150	to a UC student needing dental services
47.	$300	to a single mom who needed temporary rent assistance
48.	$300	to a CVC family whose house burned to the ground
49.	$350	to single mom for utility bills at a time of illness

50. $93   to Wes Welch for his prison ministry—books, postage
51. $200   to single mom needing grocery assistance at a time of illness
52. $60   to two couples needing premarriage counseling tests
53. $1,200   to build six $200 churches in Peru, South America
54. $500   to a Missouri family who needed job transition assistance
55. $170   to a single mom needing assistance to make ends meet
56. $300   to physician/nurse going to Africa on short-term mission trip
57. $500   to send five UC students to eXcite98 in Riverside, California
58. $60   to get a bike fitted for a handicapped man who can't drive
59. $120   to buy sweat suits for people burned out of their homes in Lincoln
60. $160   to send SS felts to 10 churches in Peru and a mission project in Tanzania
61. $300   to a single mom needing temporary housing help
62. $70   to Wes Welch for his prison ministry—books, postage
63. $225   to someone whose car had been vandalized at Halloween
64. $2,000   to partner with CVC to remodel our Something Else SS room
65. $1,100   to single moms at CVC to buy Christmas 1998 gifts for their kids
66. $550   to three community families for Christmas 1998 gifts
67. $600   to furnish a Friendship Home room at Christmas 1998

68.	$340	to help a single dad with one month's rent at Christmas 1998
69.	$150	to the Juniors for materials to make Pin One On for Josh hearts
70.	$150	to a class member needing temporary rent assistance
71.	$150	to the Good Neighbor Center for furnace replacement fund
72.	$500	to an international UC student who lost financial sponsors
73.	$100	to get bedding for a single mom and four kids whose house burned
74.	$190	to UC students going on band tour to China
75.	$250	to single mom needing auto repair assistance, plus bike and skates
76.	$120	to single mom for part of her Mexico mission trip expenses
77.	$565	to Moore, Oklahoma, Adventist Church for tornado cleanup
78.	$711	to Potter's House church plant near Red Deer, Alberta
79.	$857	to CVC youth going to Fiji mission trip
80.	$6,213	to two UC students going to India to build churches
81.	$105	to clothe children from dysfunctional home who want to attend church
82.	$65	to released prison inmate for transportation at father's sudden death
83.	$120	to Fisks at a difficult time for Josh
84.	$70	to a woman needing groceries while unemployed
85.	$47	to help a UC student with basic living supplies
86.	$158	electrical bill paid for a member of the class at a difficult time
87.	$42	to purchase food for children in a troubled home situation

88. $280   for move-in rent assistance for a single mom
89. $300   utility bill assistance for UC village student at time of surgery
90. $460   move-in rent assistance for a prisoner's spouse and baby
91. $500   CVA tuition assistance for child of single mom
92. $240   to single mom for utility bills at a time of job transition
93. $65   to UC student for basic living supplies
94. $23   for Matt Talbot Kitchen meals
95. $80   to a child in need of basic living supplies at Linda Robison's school
96. $31   to buy children's supplies for an overseas mission project
97. $157   to pay the phone bill of a class member at a difficult time
98. $125   utility bill assistance for a family at a difficult time
99. $250   Christmas 1999 gifts to a family in Hickman, Nebraska
100. $530   Christmas 1999 gifts to three families at Linda Robison's school
101. $500   Christmas 1999 gifts to two families at Janella Abby's school
102. $250   Christmas 1999 gift to people in India at Maranatha church planting project
103. $150   Christmas 1999 phone cards to former Something Else class members
104. $150   Christmas 1999 meals provided by Pathfinders to kids of single parents
105. $553   Christmas 1999 house remodeling materials for a paraplegic
106. $125   Christmas 1999 money gift to a church family at a very difficult time

107.	$100	Christmas 1999 gifts for the children of a single parent
108.	$55	Christmas 1999 for groceries going to a friend of a class member
109.	$100	Christmas 1999 to a boy in difficult circumstances in Roca, Nebraska
110.	$150	Christmas 1999 money to Saratoga School nurse for basic care kits
111.	$100	Christmas 1999 money to a single mom to buy gifts for her children
112.	$100	Christmas 1999 to help a CVC boy at the sudden death of a parent
113.	$50	Christmas 1999 gifts to children who would otherwise have nothing
114.	$85	Christmas 1999 gift to a single mom and her children
115.	$50	Christmas 1999 to UC student because she could not go home
116.	$52	for Matt Talbot Kitchen meals
117.	$395	move-in rent assistance for a family at a difficult time
118.	$200	to help a patient of one of the nurses in our class
119.	$350	to pay utility bills for a single mom
120.	$144	books to Southwestern Adventist University for students in need
121.	$34	for Matt Talbot Kitchen meals
122.	$180	to four international students for basic living supplies
123.	$150	to a single mom needing electrical bill paid
124.	$150	to a retiree who needed medication she could not afford
125.	$35	for Matt Talbot Kitchen meals
126.	$300	to help a Helen Hyatt Elementary student's school bill

127. $133   for a quadriplegic's home remodeling materials
128. $50   for Matt Talbot Kitchen meals
129. $150   to a single mom for groceries at a difficult time
130. $125   to remodel a kitchen for a woman with cancer
131. $4,000   tuition grant (Union College matched 2,000) to a dad whose son just died from lukemia
132. $450   to buy fresh fruit through the winter for Native American students at Holbrook
133. $2,385   to bring a Ugandan mother/children to the United States
134. $145   for Matt Talbot Kitchen meals
135. $98   to remodel a kitchen for a woman with cancer
136. $175   to a single mom for groceries at a difficult time
137. $100   to videotape the ministries of Something Else for General Conference session
138. $300   to a single mom for groceries and gas at a time between jobs
139. $600   for elementary school entrance fee for child from a single parent home
140. $450   to welcome 65 Union College freshmen— $7 in quarters plus laundry soap to each
141. $700   carpet for a family in which the husband was injured in a farming accident

$47,586 Total

Chapter Five

Time Ministry:

"Can You Move Chuque and Hannah Tomorrow?"

"These people just showed up and started helping me. I cried when I saw them."–an unchurched neighbor.

"We want to thank the Something Else Sabbath school class for coming to our small church and holding Sabbath school and church service."—Platte Seventh-day Adventist Church.

"To give our time to others is to say, 'I love you, and Jesus loves you' in a way that everyone understands."—Marlyn Schwartz.

IN A TIME-CRUNCHED, time-starved society, our time is perhaps the most precious gift we can offer. One of our goals is to make Sabbath school a place where people know we care enough that they can call us *whenever* they need extra hands. Another goal is to remind ourselves that our busyness will not keep us from taking time to help others.

Time ministry has reached many people who aren't Adventists. We've been blessed by getting to know some people we've helped; others we'll probably never meet again. Periodically we help one of our own members, as with Joshua Fisk, whose parents, Greg and Anita, are members of Something Else.

We started praying for 7-year-old Josh when his leukemia reoccurred. Friends informed us of some financial needs the Fisks would incur because of hospital bills, so our class helped through prayer and money ministries for several months. During that time little Josh endured a bone marrow transplant and a long recovery. After a welcome remission Josh was able to return to the Adventist elementary school and be with his friends again.

About three years passed before the cancer returned. When it did, we again held Josh up in prayer. This time his immune system was so weak that the doctors recommended he stay away from other children to avoid catching their illnesses.

Here was a tough predicament. Anita, Josh's mother, operated a children's day-care center from their home. She needed to keep working, because Greg attended classes full-time toward a physician's assistant degree at Union College. They considered turning their garage into a separate bedroom for Josh, but they had no idea where the funds or the labor would come from. However, Anita did get a picture in her mind of someone in our class, Marlyn Schwartz, who knows construction.

Marlyn also happens to be the person who heads up our time ministry program. Upon receiving Anita's call, he began placing telephone calls. People in the community along with class members began donating labor and materials, and within a week the Fisk garage had been converted into a beautiful bedroom for Josh.

Marlyn's wife, Sharon, even managed to obtain a basketball personally signed by Josh's sports hero, Michael Jordan.

The story appeared on the local television news, touching the hearts of many viewers. A trust fund was established to help with Josh's medical expenses. When Josh transferred in and out of the hospital for many months, members of our class organized shifts to help out with food and baby-sitting. Our prayers continued to ascend.

We all have the same number of hours in a day; how we choose to use our time is up to each individual. As Jesus walked this earth, He spent His time as the great healer and joy giver, often stopping to heal someone emotionally as well as physically. Likewise, some of the busiest people we know are the ones who will stop and help us when we are in real need.

What happened to Josh? His cancer took over, and Josh died last year. On his bed he whispered his last words to his dad: "I love God . . . more than anything."

We know we were like family to Josh and his family during his illness. And our class continues to be supportive even now. Greg recalls, "When my son Joshua was sick with leukemia, the Something Else class came out and funded, organized, and turned our garage into a bedroom for my son. It was amazing. They really live what they preach."

ONE CLASS AND A TRUCK

We have helped many families move during the past few years. If you have ever moved, you know what a huge job it is. Strong hands and backs are appreciated, even if you have no idea whom they belong to. As Sharon

Pitcher noted, "Often our Sabbath school class helps people move, even some that aren't Adventist. We organize right there in class, give the times and addresses, and find out who can make it."

One Sabbath morning our prayer time ran a little longer, and we had many announcements, so Chris forgot to ask for a show of hands to see who could help Chuque and Hannah move. Chuque and Hannah were special to us because they had been class members since the very beginning of Something Else. We had known them as students, then later as husband and wife. Now they were moving to Colorado to begin new jobs.

That Saturday night we realized, with great gnashing of teeth, that we hadn't organized to help our friends move. Chris made some hurried phone calls to see who could help pack Chuque and Hannah the following morning. Would anyone show with such short notice?

Two weeks later the class received a postcard from Colorado. Hannah wrote, "We attended this class for the past four and a half years, and we always knew you were 'Something Else.' Yet, a week ago Sunday, you proved it to us one last time by showing up at our house to help load our moving van. You had us completely packed and on the road by 1:00 p.m. You're Something Else! Thanks for everything—we miss you already."

That Sunday morning more people had shown up than we could believe. Sabbath school members swarmed the house and yard. Al, a UPS driver, packed everything perfectly—including the chain-link fence.

Time ministries also operates on a continuous basis. Our longest-running ministry is Matt Talbot Kitchen, a soup kitchen for the homeless. One Sabbath morning a month Vicki and Ron Biloff take a group of about 10 people to feed 60-95 people. Vicki purchases the food during the week, and sometimes the dessert is made and donated by church members. The food is served on tables with tablecloths and real silverware. Everyone is treated with dignity and respect. Often students or younger children serve the dessert, and the people are warmed by seeing the younger people and talking with them. It has been a wonderful ministry, one that the Biloffs have been so faithful in doing.

Another one of Ron's ministries is his flower ministry. He brings a couple dozen flowers to class and lets members take them to shut-ins, visitors, or friends. We attach a card to the flower stem that says, "From your Something Else Sabbath school friends." People are so surprised when they are given a flower and it isn't even a special holiday. Some Sabbaths we can look across the congregation and see a garden of bright colors. It's fun to see how one person with a creative idea can spread joy throughout a congregation.

Each fall our Christmas family and wrapping ministry locates needy families. We collect money over several weeks and find out if the families need specific items such as clothing, small appliances, or toys. At times we have given food or gift certificates. After the money is collected and the gifts are bought in a huge shopping spree, our class holds a wrapping party (where we play "wrap music") after a Sabbath potluck. The wrapping is organized so that some people box the gifts, some people wrap, and others put name tags on.

Children love to help with the wrapping, and the brightly colored gifts are delivered to the families' homes by members of our class. Members come back and describe the sometimes horrible living conditions and stories of joy from the families who received the presents. This has been an annual tradition that our class eagerly looks forward to. Last year we raised an amazing $3,290 over six offerings to help 18 families.

We have other time ministries, such as our lemonade stand that we set up one hot Sabbath afternoon on a bike path. People were surprised when we offered them free lemonade without one "catch" (not even a Bible text at the bottom of the cup). Every year we gather in December on a Friday night to go out caroling, then come back to the church for hot chocolate and cookies. We have shoveled snow for people and refurbished a kitchen for a woman who has cancer. Moreover, we send out "missionaries" to help with our church's junior, earliteen, and youth Sabbath schools for two or three years at a time. The projects are endless.

Some time ministry principles to keep in mind:

1. Projects should be a class decision.

2. Give consideration to all projects brought before the class.

3. Pray for God's leading. Stay nimble and responsive.

4. Don't expect anything more than joy in return.

Again, please adapt these ideas. Use them as they fit, and take time to watch the love grow.

"Thank you so much for your help in taking care of the renovations in our house. It turned out great. All of your support and prayers since my accident have made this very difficult time a lot easier. God bless you all!"

Chapter Six

Study Ministry:

"Why Do You Always Ask Questions?"

"Our prayer time, as well as our money and time ministries, build a community. By the time we get to the lesson study portion of the morning, we're able to quickly dive into the Word. We know each other already, so we talk deeply about things that matter to us."—Kathy Bollinger.

"What I appreciate about Something Else study time is how we wed theory with practical application to our lives. Each Sabbath I'm blessed by at least one new awareness of God; on a special day, half a dozen shimmering insights blaze their way into my consciousness. How is this possible? Lesson study is supposed to be dry as the hills of Gilboa. Here I eagerly look forward to each week."–Buell Fogg.

THE AUTHORS OF this book are both professional educators, so this section could run 700 pages. Don't worry. Countless books and ideas have already been written on effective teaching, so we'll concentrate on the basics of study ministry basics. (By "effective teaching" we mean teaching that *changes* lives.)

"Making disciples" comes about through all of the five ministries of a ministry-driven Sabbath school. How can our study of the Word of God best accomplish discipling?

Here are four practical study ministry tips.

1. While discussing the topic, use a whiteboard to drive points home visually. We view a whiteboard, erasable markers, and an eraser as essential ministry-driven study equipment. Most people are visual learners. Even if you must wheel a portable whiteboard in and out of the church sanctuary, for the sake of learning and community, do it.*

Suppose, for example, you're examining Luke 2:41-52, the account of the boy Jesus in the Temple. Your class discussion could run in many directions:

Why did Joseph and Mary lose sight of Jesus?

What does it mean to be "in my Father's house"? Can we be "there" also when we're outside a church building? Could it be possible that we aren't "in His house" even when we're sitting in church? What gets in the way? What enables you to be in the Father's presence, no matter where you are?

If you decide to pursue the first question using an extrabiblical source, you might start with Ellen White's comment from *The Desire of Ages:* "If Joseph and Mary had stayed their minds upon God by meditation and prayer, they would have realized the sacredness of their trust, and would not have lost sight of Jesus. By one day's neglect they lost the Saviour; but it cost them three days of anxious search to find Him. So with us; by idle talk, evilspeaking, or neglect of prayer, we may in one day lose the Saviour's presence, and it may take many days of sorrowful search to find Him, and regain the peace that we have lost" (p. 83).

That's a mouthful. You could go back to the text, or pursue the next questions. But imagine now that you turn to the whiteboard and write:

1. idle talk
2. evil speaking
3. neglect of prayer

By writing these down, you focus. Instantly you have enough material for an entire session. The application portion of this lesson can change lives. Defining terms will lead to interesting distinctions. Does "talk" and "speaking" also include *listening?* Where might entertainment fit in here?

And what about "losing His presence" when Jesus promises never to leave us? What is it that we lose? How will we know when we've got "it" back?

Note that this questioning tendency is not inherently a doubting attitude. Questions lead us to deeper discoveries, treasures, epiphanies, changes. Christians today tend to provide answers and preach proof texts; Jesus asked questions and told stories.

A learned rabbi was once asked by a student, "Why do you always ask questions?"

The rabbi replied, "Is there something wrong with that?"

Of course, we seek the answers, the way, the truth, the life. First, though, we must feel our need and ask the questions. Writing important insights on a board brings them home to us, so that we aren't anxiously searching for days to find the point.

2. Involve everyone as much as possible. Following "neighbor nudging" (we will explain this later), you may break into small groups of four to six. Ask the person with the curliest hair in each group to be the spokesperson. This person will take notes and announce the group's findings to the class. Give each group a different question. Such an approach encourages maximum participation and enables the discussion to achieve more depth and scope.

We also involve as many teachers as possible. Sharing teaching responsibilities from week to week lightens the teaching load, provides variety, and allows more to participate in leadership. We make spaces for guest teachers occasionally. Common objections of "too much commitment" dissolve when we distribute the load.

3. Have fun. In *Who Switched the Price Tags?* Tony Campolo contends: "There isn't anything frivolous about having fun. Learning how to have fun is one of the most serious subjects in the world. Without fun, marriages don't work. When jobs aren't fun, they become intolerable and dehumanizing. When children aren't fun, they are heartbreaking. When church is not fun, religion becomes a drag. When life is not fun, it is hard to be spiritual."

One way to enable fun to occur in your study is to use props. Purchase pipe cleaners for the class (tap into our kinesthetic learning mode). Ask them to shape a symbol of God's peace and explain what their symbol means. Use a Nerf ball to toss to the next speaker. That will keep people awake! Why should the kids have all the movement, color, and fun?

Fun is attractive. Fun is the chocolate chips in the cookie dough of religion. Even when discussing Adventist fundamentals, however, without the "fun" we are left with merely "da mentals"—that is, theoretical, lifeless knowledge. We must do better.

4. Choose study materials that meet your needs. You may choose to use standard lesson quarterlies or create your own study schedules. We have done both. For the past two years we have created our own Scripture study schedule. (See Appendix C for a sample.) Using a Sabbath school quarterly can work superbly as well, and is easier on some visitors.

These four tips have worked for us. Finally, apply the following artful approach to study ministry.

CALLING AAA!

Ask. If the teacher begins with a lecture, discussion will be difficult to come by later. The first and best way to generate discussion is to start with "neighbor nudging." This technique calls for people to turn to a partner and discuss a personal question for two minutes and 14 seconds (a round "two minutes" usually expands to 10). An apt neighbor-nudging question to open discussion on our lesson would be: "Share a time you or a family member was lost. What happened?" You can refer to these responses later.

Many people who are afraid to speak up in front of everyone will chatter like a chipmunk to one person. The atmosphere of the class warms up immediately. Then you may ask two or three people *what they heard* their partner say. This encourages listening and discourages stage hogging. Also, gently make it known that *no more personal stories will be told until the "apply" section*. This may seem harsh, but it keeps everyone on task.

Probably 90 percent of a study leader's job should be to ask questions that connect thoughts. Take pains to ask those questions that we all think but rarely verbalize. For example, when discussing the boy Jesus at the Temple, ask the question everyone is really thinking: "Do you, deep down, think that Jesus was really disrespectful to His parents? How would you react to your child if you searched a day for him and he said that?"

Then be prepared for follow-up questions, such as "What's the difference between your child and Jesus as a boy?" "How are all children like the child Jesus?" "Would your irritation be tempered if you at last found your child in front of TV cameras, with seasoned journalists sitting around him, in awe at your child's magnificent wisdom and maturity?"

Open-ended questions, ones that cannot be answered with one or two words, are best for discussion. Deepening levels of discussion, from simple to profound, can be prompted by the first word in our question. The deeper questions often begin with "How," "Why," and "What if."

Analyze. Here is where the class considers *context*. Don't "retell" entire Bible stories. (Most students can read them just fine.) Instead, take the opportunity to concentrate on the most pithy and poignant points. Look at original meanings of words. Compare scripture with scripture.

For example, Luke 2:46 and 47 says: "After three days they found him in the temple, sitting among the teachers, listening to them and asking them questions; and all who heard him were amazed at his understanding and his answers." Notice that Jesus did as a boy what he would do the rest of His life: He listened and asked questions before providing answers.

Turn to the end of Luke, to chapter 24, to the famous walk to Emmaus. Here we find a few parallels. After three days, when Jesus was "lost," the travelers found Him again. "And he said to them, 'What is this conversation which you are holding with each other as you walk?' And they stood still, looking sad."

How many times are we sad, and Jesus draws near, longing to heal us? He asks questions and listens. Then He opens the Scriptures to us while our hearts burn within. And we share the exciting news with others, as the Emmaus travelers did with the eleven disciples.

But sometimes we are like Mary, His mother, who "kept all these things in her heart" (Luke 2:51). "These things" provide an inner fire that we can feed from and warm to when the embers of our faith threaten to grow cold.

Wouldn't it be good to stay in the Word just to keep looking at Jesus?

As a class we purchased hardback Bibles and embossed "Something Else Sabbath School" on the covers. These are handed out at the beginning of lesson study to anyone who needs a Bible. The name on the cover helps to ensure that the Bibles remain here for future students of Scripture.

One of the most powerful parts of a lesson is a healthy silence. Resist the urge to "rescue" all discussion after three seconds of silence. In silence we can think for ourselves. God speaks to us in the silence.

Apply. Examples, examples, examples. We have used examples here in sharing our approach to study ministry. What would this section be like without examples? The same is true for your lesson studies.

Connect to reality. Ask: "How can you practically apply this lesson to your life?" "What changes will you make?" Enter the affective domain—talk about emotions, frustrations, hopes, fears. Remind the class that by His word He can calm all storms.

Finally, summarize the main points on the board.

Sometimes we close with a simple, beautiful a capella song. That's one way we make certain our study ends on a good note.

"Keep reminding them of these things. Warn them before God against quarreling about words; it is of no value and only ruins those who listen. Do your best to present yourself to God as one approved, a workman who does not need to be ashamed and who correctly handles the word of truth" (2 Timothy 2:14, 15, NIV).

––––––

* We keep a small, lockable filing cabinet to store markers, the prayer card box, and other necessities.

Chapter Seven

Social Ministry:

"We Are Family—Don't Forget It"

"The social aspect of this class should not be underrated. Knowing each other on more intimate levels is what puts a face on the church."—Mark Robison.

JESUS WAS A social person. He socialized at weddings, dinner parties, on walks, in boats, within houses, large and small. He liked being with people to the point that the Pharisees complained about His social nature.

Later, the early Christian church "devoted themselves to the apostles' teaching and fellowship, to the breaking of bread and the prayers. . . . And day by day, attending the temple together and breaking bread in their homes, they partook of food with glad and generous hearts, praising God and having favor with all the people" (Acts 2:42-27).

Several months after Something Else had been meeting we felt a need to socialize outside of class, to get to know individuals on a more personal level. We started doing two significant things. First, we planned a potluck (Chris calls them *potgoodlucks*), which was organized by members of the class. Potgoodlucks have continued on a regular basis ever since.

We also have added Sabbath school brunches, to which families bring a breakfast food: fruit, muffins, hash browns, coffee cake, or juice. These take place once or twice a year and are planned by our social committee. Our brunches are scheduled in the classroom a half hour before Sabbath school officially begins.

Second, we began something we call simply "interviews." Prior to Sabbath mornings Chris will ask someone if it's all right if he calls them in front of the class to ask questions about themselves, their family, their work, or any other questions of interest. Over the years we have done many interviews, and people in the class have appreciated these five-minute sessions. Class members often comment on how they were surprised to learn something new about someone they already knew. It has also worked as a springboard for further conversations with that individual or couple.

Soon after the potgoodlucks and interviews were started, we began putting together our "You're Something Else" bulletin board. Pictures of all class members were taken with a Polaroid camera, and when the film was developed Teri (our first photographer) placed the pictures on the bulletin board with the members' names. Not only was it fun to see how the pictures turned out, but as the class grew we were able to identify the new people attending. The film was purchased with our class money, and Teri faithfully made her camera available each week. After class those whose pictures were not yet on our board would meet Teri at a designated spot to have their picture taken.

We continue our picture board even now and find visitors intrigued by the concept and by the warmth it brings to the class. Currently we're looking into using a digital camera so that we can place pictures on a Web site and electronic newsletter. In addition, we're planning a pop quiz to match class members' names with pictures. This should be a great surprise, unless they're reading this.

As our class size grew we discovered that we needed a more organized social ministry. We passed around a sheet for people to sign up to be on the social committee, asked for names and phone numbers, and picked a time to hold our first formal meeting. At that first meeting of eight people we chose a leader, Charlotte, who is organized and as a longtime resident in Lincoln had cultivated good resources.

During the next six months the social committee brainstormed possible activities to take place. Then we assigned different people to follow through with whatever needed to be done. We worked mostly in teams of two, knowing we could also call on other members of the committee. The various activities were assigned a month and a specific date. Charlotte followed through with typing out the social schedule and made sure everyone received a copy the following week. This committee still meets every six months to brainstorm ideas and outline activities for the class.

Some annual socials have proved to be favorites. One is our Waubonsie State Park Sabbath school and church outing every autumn. Waubonsie is about 60 miles from Lincoln, so class members' families and friends carpool to this beautiful park when the leaves have turned bright orange, red, and yellow. We meet at a clearing with picnic tables and easy access to walking paths around the park. Sabbath school starts with singing for all ages, prayer, and some kind of innovative, spirited game that Kathy creates to involve everyone (usually split into two teams: "boys" versus "girls"). After Sabbath school we move right into church. Usually, we have a few announcements, a song or special music, and a guest speaker.

After church we set up for potgoodluck, socializing, and discussing the sermon we just experienced. Many families look forward to this day because it's a time to experience the outdoors and be with God and friends in such a refreshing way. In the afternoon many choose to take a hike to the "lookout" (about 200 feet above the plains) while others prefer to stay in their chairs or on their blankets to visit. It's a wonderful annual tradition.

Our yearly social activities calendar looked like this for 1999:

January 22	Friday night vespers; speaker, John Harris
February 13	Sabbath school brunch
March 6	Sabbath school potgoodluck
April 10	Bowling on Saturday night
May 1	Cantrells' farewell potgoodluck
July 4	Picnic supper and fireworks
July 30	Miniature golf and worship
August 28	Woodland Acres vespers; speaker, Chris Blake
September 17	Annual hot dog roast and vespers; speaker, Sharon Pitcher
October 9	Annual Waubonsie State Park Sabbath school and church; speaker, Andy Nash
December 20	Christmas caroling
December 21	Sabbath school potgoodluck and wrapping presents for needy families

The activities center on class needs, interests, and availability. Every other year we take over a local health club late on Saturday night and play for hours. And of course, if we had an ocean within three hours of us, that would provide another option. "Surf Nebraska" hasn't caught on yet.

One memorable social activity was ROIL ("Reaching Out in Love"), which took place during 1997 and 1998. ROIL started with the Richardsons, who had experienced it in a former church and saw what joy and fun it brought to all who participated. The rules are on the Center for Creative Ministry Web site (see Appendix A), along with some sample letters you may use.

The activity begins with one family ROILing two other families and then doubling from there until everyone in the class has been ROILed. Gifts and notes are mysteriously left for a week without the receiving family knowing who has left them. We encouraged members to leave inexpensive and creative gifts: homemade bread, a candle, a small book or plant. Gifts are placed on people's doorsteps, at their work, or sometimes delivered by a neighbor. In the middle of the week an invitation asks the family to have dinner with their secret host, and at that time it's revealed who has been "Reaching Out in Love."

As the group grew we ended up holding dinners at the church fellowship hall. Many great stories were told about the secret deliveries, the frantic escapes, and the call to the police bomb squad to disarm a teapot in a cardboard box.

KEEPING IN TOUCH

Chris has always wanted to stay in touch with people who have come to Something Else. One of our first lists for keeping track of members looked like this:

1. Have greeters at the door to show hospitality. Encourage members to sit toward the front.

2. Update a guest list so we can send newsletters and quick thank-you notes to visitors.

3. Make phone calls to members absent several Sabbaths in a row to let them know they are missed.

4. Keep updated membership list to provide accurate information for possible prayer chain.

5. Send "missed seeing you" cards to members.

Justin and Heather were the first couple to make a checklist of all the members. However, as they tried to keep track, they found it an overwhelming job for two people.

Then a member (and our pastor's wife) came forward with some super ideas. Cindy is a problem solver and an organizer, and she formed a format for keeping track of members called "People Discipleship Strategies," which is what we use today. Perhaps most important, Cindy set up goals—and the means to meet those goals. We're never listless when Cindy is in charge.

SOMETHING ELSE SOCIAL MINISTRY GOALS

A balanced Sabbath school and church will anticipate, promote, and provide for social needs. These strategies have helped us keep closer track of members and visitors, as well as enhance our class communication.

A   Keep current, updated record of members by circulating class list every six months

B.   Regular contact with members who miss Sabbath school

Follow-up postcards, cards, phone calls,

        bulletins to those missing

C. Incorporate visitors quickly

        Have greeters at the door each week—
           one person is in charge of scheduling

        Friendship dinners—members from our class
           sign up to invite visitors and class
           members to potluck in their homes

D. Communication

        Update our "You're Something Else" bulletin
           board with pictures of every member

        Keep our Something Else Web site current

        Develop a brochure for visitors that shares
           what our class is about

        Produce a quarterly newsletter for informa-
           tion updates and short, inspiring articles

        Use e-mail for announcements and prayer
           requests during the week.

We are still honing many of these—we have not "arrived" by any means. But we constantly try to demonstrate that everyone—*every one*—is a member of our family, and should be prized, stretched, and encouraged in redemptive ways. As one person remarked after being ROILed: "I felt as if someone really cared about me."

Perhaps that's the best definition of social ministry.

Chapter Eight

Starting Your Ministry-driven Sabbath School:

"If Not Now, When?"

RECENTLY WE RECEIVED a forwarded e-message entitled "Dumb Packaging Labels." Included in the list of actual label instructions on consumer goods:

1. On some Swanson frozen dinners: "Serving suggestions: Defrost."

2. On most brands of Christmas lights: "For indoor or outdoor use only."

3. On Sainsbury's peanuts: "Warning: Contains nuts."

4. On a bag of Fritos: "You could be a winner! No purchase necessary. Details inside."

5. On a bottle of All laundry detergent: "Remove clothing before distributing in washing machine."

Unfortunately, absurd labels can bring more than smiles. Some labels damage, overwhelm, taint, crush.

"Conservative."

"Radical."

"Liberal."

What a tragedy when God's body becomes riddled with toxic tags. Fortunately, we can—as Jesus did and does—live beyond labels.

Ministry-driven Sabbath school members are conservative radicals with liberal applications.

Conservative: We long to preserve the fragrance of Christ. As Ellen White says, "Christianity is always intensely practical." The disciple John declares, "God is love" (1 John 4:8). James also points out a faith fundamental: "If a brother or sister is ill-clad and in lack of daily food, and one of you says to them, 'Go in peace, be warmed and filled,' without giving them the things needed for the body, what does it profit?" (James 1:15, 16). We must keep on defending that which is basic, true, noble.

Radical: The literal meaning of "radical" is "to the root," which is where Jesus always moved. Whether with a Samaritan woman at a well or a learned Pharisee under cover of night, Jesus cut to the root to connect directly with real needs. He was never an extremist; His life was always graciously radical.

Liberal: God affixed to His gospel one label: "Directions: To be applied liberally." When we love generously without regard for external barriers we become like Jesus, the world's greatest lover. We disciples are called to love like Him who could not stop giving. Thus we are liberally filled with His joy, peace, and hope.

Conservative, radical, liberal Christians can bear any labels people place on us because we know that God sees the label on our hearts. The one that says "I belong to Jesus."

THEREFORE, MAKE DISCIPLES

Ministry-driven Sabbath schools also belong to Jesus. These ministry-driven Sabbath schools will bring healing to churches ripped apart by name-calling and divisive factions.

Have you ever noticed how bickering and infighting stops when people work together for something important? Unify to react heroically when the river overflows or a child is trapped beneath rubble after an earthquake. They don't care about superficial labels.

Every church needs that unifying sense of urgency. Unfortunately, we become blind to urgent needs that exist every day. These urgent needs live down the block, across the ocean, even in front of us in church. They need our prayers, our money, our time, our wisdom, our friendship.

But as Gottfried Oosterwal writes in *Mission: Possible:*

"After we have taken our oath of allegiance in baptism, whereby we pledged to participate in the great controversy between Christ and Satan, we either went AWOL, or we remained in the barracks, becoming more and more refined in the use of God's armor but never leaving our Christian camp to fight for the restoration of God's kingdom. Under these circumstances, no wonder battles soon break out in the barracks" (p. 111).

We must fight against becoming insulated from the world instead of inoculated to enter the world. We must believe that the apples surest to go bad are those that never get out of the barrel. In his magnificent prayer of John 17, Jesus says, "I do not pray that you should take them out of the world. . . . As you sent Me into the world, I also have sent them into the world" (verses 15-18, NKJV). This is a call to *action*. That's why we have emblazoned these words in foot-high letters at the front of our Something Else classroom: "THE KINGDOM OF GOD DOES NOT CONSIST IN TALK BUT IN POWER" (1 Cor. 4:20).

Ministry-driven Sabbath schools are havens of present truth. As Ellen White proclaims:

"Present truth, from the first letter of its alphabet to

the last, means missionary effort" *(Counsels on Health,* p. 300). And though Jesus never crossed an ocean or learned a foreign language, she rightly calls Him "the greatest missionary the world has ever known" *(Welfare Ministry,* p. 118).

After our first six years at Something Else, we know that something even better lies ahead. We don't know precisely what it is, what opportunities God has in store—starting a literacy center, interacting with a Messianic Jewish congregation, or helping plant ministry-driven Sabbath schools in Lincoln, Valparaiso, or Seattle. We eagerly follow His leading into the future.

If God is calling you to begin this Sabbath school ministry, you need to be unswerving in your commitment to follow Him.

You also need practical steps to begin. Reading this book is one step, of course, but now what? Rather than burying you under a mountain of advice, we refer you back to the five simple instructions in chapter one:

1. Recognize that ministry-driven classes aren't for everybody. Lead your church only as far as it is ready to go right now. Stretch the members, but not so far that you are perceived as an enemy instead of a friend. When you hit a rough patch, hold on to what you have gained (don't go back to Egypt), and when the time seems right, move forward again. Be unfailingly gracious.

2. Adapt ideas to your situation. Determine what vision and strategies God has in mind for your class. Plenty of resources are available to achieve this important step. *See the appendixes that follow* for information about communication, training, and material support. Become well acquainted with this support resource.

3. Begin with a Christ-centered core of believers.

Talk to friends and acquaintances that you believe may be open to starting a ministry-driven Sabbath school. Never take rejection of your ideas personally. Share copies of this book with these people and decide on a time to meet afterward to make specific plans. Be humble enough to take directions and change course. You are not the true leader of this class. Jesus is.

Also, conduct a needs assessment survey of your church members. Talk to key people and ask searching questions about what is needed, what will succeed, where the land mines may lie. Then poll the appropriate groups to determine their hopes and dreams for a new activist Sabbath school. Once you have the information, believe it.

4. Pray, pray, pray. Though you may be working as hard as a one-handed accordion player, you will do no great thing for God without prayer. As Howard Hendricks asserts: "Show me an individual who is effective in public, and I will show you an individual who is effective in private. Find a person of deep conviction who is genuinely impacting his society, and you'll inevitably find a person who spends time alone with God."

Gather your core believers to pray. Include as many as possible into your prayer circle.

5. Get ready for adventure. You will experience highs and lows, assault and flattery, unexpected people picking up the ball and others dropping it, astonishing turns of events. God is eternally surprising. John Burroughs writes, "For anything worth having one must pay the price; and the price is always work, patience, love, self-sacrifice."

Remember Jesus' promise: "I am with you always, to the close of the age."

Enjoy the journey. Go with God.

Support for Ministry-driven Sabbath Schools

By Paul Richardson, Director
Center for Creative Ministry

IF YOU HAVE ever tried to start anything significant, you have a good idea how much planning, persistence, and prayer it takes to pull it off effectively. We hope that by the time you have reached this point in the book you are saying to yourself, "I think we could start a ministry-driven Sabbath school in our church."

In the years since the Something Else Sabbath school started in Lincoln, numerous groups of people have met with us and then gone back home to implement the same program in their church. Some have experienced exceptional success; others have run headlong into obstacles they never expected.

The Center for Creative Ministry is fully recognized by the Seventh-day Adventist Church as a leader in innovative ministry. For more than 13 years the center has provided leading-edge resources that are field-tested to reach new generations of church leaders. In addition, the center is the coordinator of the Reconnecting Ministries of the North American Division, where we build and support a network of friends reaching friends who have quit coming to church. As you plan, persist, and pray about your ministry-driven Sabbath school, know that you have plenty of support. Here's how much.

COMMUNICATION SUPPORT

You will find that talking with others who have started a ministry-driven Sabbath school is invaluable. How do you find these people? Simply contact the Center for Creative Ministry (information later in this appendix). This resource center keeps a current list of ministry-driven Sabbath schools, the contact persons at each location, and how to reach each one. We initiate links to Web sites developed by the various ministry-driven Sabbath schools around the world. In addition, we sponsor forums in which networking can take place and new ideas for these Sabbath schools are generated.

Twenty-four-hour support is available through our Web site: www.creativeministry.org. This site includes many free items helpful to your Sabbath school as well as an online store with items that can quickly be shipped right to your door. The Web site also includes a chat room for ministry-driven Sabbath schools.

TRAINING SUPPORT

Often for a visually oriented church member, seeing is believing. So first, purchase copies of this book to distribute to those whom you think might be open to participating in a ministry-driven Sabbath school. Next, request from the Center for Creative Ministry a specially made video that *shows* the five ministries of Something Else Sabbath school in action. This video also presents interviews and step-by-step directions.

Frequently we receive calls asking one of the leaders from an effective class to visit a new setting.

Starting a ministry-driven Sabbath school may require a consultant from "the outside" to win participants over to this new approach. Contact our office for an information packet on what it takes to have training take place at your church.

MATERIAL SUPPORT

Want to know more about spiritual gifts in your church, ROIL, effective small groups, or reaching the unchurched? Resources on these and more subjects are available through the Center for Creative Ministry. To request our catalog or receive other support, contact:

Center for Creative Ministry
2935 Pine Lake Road, Suite J
Lincoln, NE 68516-6009
1.800.272.4664 (phone in United States and Canada)
1.402.420.7710 (phone)
1.402.437.9502 (facsimile)
www.creativeministry.org (Web site)

FINAL THOUGHTS

Too many times leaders look for the latest and greatest materials, thinking they are just what their group needs to be effective. Not necessarily so. Many good initiatives from Church A have fallen flat at Church B. We encourage you to adapt all ministry-driven concepts to fit the needs of your particular church. Make sure not to work in isolation. After you have received support in getting started, tell others about your ministry-driven Sabbath school and help them start one. This simple but significant step of getting involved outside its circle will revolutionize your class.

Share this book and the video with other interested

people and introduce them to the support you now know is available. There is plenty of encouragement for your pioneering work. Together we're making a difference as we start ministry-driven Sabbath schools!

Something Else in Cedar Lake, Michigan

By Robert Jensen

AFTER HEARING ABOUT ministry-driven Sabbath schools, I was so incredibly inspired by the idea. It seemed to be a concept that answered many of the nagging doubts I had been harboring for some time about the practicality of Sabbath school. But it still took me three months of praying and wrestling with the idea before I got up the nerve to talk to our pastor about it. This was such a unique approach that I doubted that anyone here would be open to the idea.

Finally I promised the Lord that if He would open up a way, I would follow His lead and do what I could to initiate the program at Cedar Lake. After meeting with all the proper levels of organization (pastor, Sabbath school superintendent, Sabbath school council, church board) we were given permission to try it for six months. I drew up some principles for the class:

It's not about:	*It's about:*
Being different	Making a difference
Being entertained	Being inspired
Being comfortable	Being challenged
Being a spectator	Being a participant

So we started our class on the first Sabbath of July

1999. After six months we reported back to the church board. The response was overwhelmingly in favor. In fact, the response from the entire church has been positive. I cannot recall even one negative comment. In addition, they are starting to incorporate some of our ideas or style into other church functions.

Our Something Else Sabbath school starts at 9:15 a.m. and goes until 10:45 a.m. We begin with a 30-minute musical praise session, then move to a 15-minute prayer time (for which we keep a list of answered prayers), and a 15-minute period for service projects, including time and money ministries. We conclude with a 30-minute study session. So far the two most popular times are praise time and prayer time.

Weekly attendance averages 30 to 35, with ages ranging from 10 to 60. Our class seems to be the place that many former and/or nonattending Adventists are being drawn to.

I continue to pray for God's leading. It is difficult and sometimes discouraging to try to get people to move out of their comfort zones, especially those of my generation. The fact that we have a large percentage of young people helps—they are not set in their ways yet.

Keep us on your prayer list, and you will be on ours.

Appendix C

Bible Study for Something Else Sabbath School

(Read ahead! Bring your Bible, questions, and comments.)

Jesus' Sermon on the Mount
First Quarter 2000

January 1	Matthew 5:21-26 (sixth commandment)
January 8	Matthew 5:27-37 (seventh commandment)
January 15	Matthew 5:38-48 (retaliation and love)
January 22	Matthew 6:1-15 (piety and power)
January 29	Matthew 6:16-18 (fasting and appearances)
February 5	Matthew 6:19-21, 24 (riches)
February 12	Matthew 6:22, 23 (light or darkness)
February 19	Matthew 6:25-34 (worry)
February 26	Matthew 7:1-6 (censure and reproof)
March 4	Matthew 7:7-12 (asking in prayer and golden rule)
March 11	Matthew 7:13,14 (narrow and wide gates)
March 18	Matthew 7:15-20 (false prophets)
March 25	Matthew 7:21-29 (profession and possession)

Prayer Brought Me Home

By Mark Robison

I KNEW I had found a home when I volunteered to pray for someone else's prayer request.

My wife, Linda, and I had recently moved to Lincoln from the Pacific Northwest. We loved the College View church service but were looking within this fairly large congregation for a way to connect on a personal level. We had attended Something Else and had attended a couple other Sabbath school classes while comparison shopping. This Something Else class seemed to provide an environment in which we could put down spiritual roots and grow, yet we continued to feel like outsiders. We were the new kids at school.

Ironically, the class at that time was praying faithfully week after week for a couple who had moved from Lincoln to Phoenix and were lonely, desperately seeking a church home. Each time the request was (once more) put on the board, Linda and I would stiffen a little and roll our eyes, wanting to yell out, "Hey! We're right here. We can show you lonely!"

We hung in there.

About the fifth week a different type of prayer request dropped with a thud into the class. A parent, friend to one of the class members, had backed out of her driveway that week, had not seen her toddler walking behind the automobile, and had run over the child, killing him.

A mother had run over her own child.

We all sat stunned.

No one was raising a hand to volunteer for this prayer. I knew it was mine to pray.

I could still hear the beating of the blades and the swirling dust as the Life Flight helicopter arrived at the school where I had taught in Washington State. One of the bus drivers, a mother who kept her 2-year-old son in a car seat behind her as she drove her rounds, had just returned from a sixth-grade field trip. The bus was emptied, she was only pulling slowly through the parking lot to the gas pump, her toddler standing on the seat behind her, grasping the lowered window. The bus encountered a speed bump, which even at that slow speed jounced the child high and through the window to tumble under the rear wheel of the bus.

A mother had run over her own child.

I raised my hand. I don't remember much of what I said in that prayer except that I gave to God on behalf of those two mothers all the What ifs and If onlys they must be feeling still, and I prayed for the peace of God to come upon us all.

And come upon me it did. By praying for someone else's pain, I felt connected to those around me, even to the couple in Phoenix. I knew I had come home.